A Pocket Guide to

How To

Hula

edited by
Patricia Lei Anderson Murray

photographs by
Joe Perrone

*C*ontents

*I*ntroduction

The words "lovely *hula* hands" bring to mind the romance of palms swaying on moonlit beaches and waves crashing on golden sand—an enchanting notion perpetuated for decades by Hawai'i's songwriters, singers, and dancers for the millions who visit the fair islands of Hawai'i. Graceful *hula* hands, accompanied by swaying bodies adorned with fragrant flowers, have mesmerized many into believing that *hula* was only an alluring dance that steals away the heart of anyone fortunate enough to experience it.

But behind the *hula*'s romance are historic visions of the sacred life-giving qualities that were so meaningful to the Hawaiians—the importance of *'ohana*, family, of the *'aina*, or land, and the treasures provided by them. Hawaiians danced to celebrate life and express gratitude for the abundance that was theirs. They danced for the birth of their children, for gifts of nature, and especially to honor ancestors. Hawaiians expressed life through the poetry and passion of dance. Children and loved ones were described in song and dance as rare scented flowers plucked from green mountain peaks. Dances that told of flowers and *lei* were really referring to children and loved ones.

Early Hawaiian history was once only oral history, since there was no written language until the missionaries introduced one. The *oli* or chant, along with the *hula*, were ways of telling one's life story, recounting genealogies and narrating history. Besides a major storytelling vehicle of Hawaiian life, the hula was also a sacred religious art form danced by a privileged and highly-regarded few, and used to teach, preserve and carry on ancient traditions for future generations.

Early visitors and newcomers to Hawai'i created their own interpretations of the *hula*. Missionaries saw the *hula* as vulgar and considered it a symptom of a degrading lifestyle lived by Hawaiians. Because of their negative view, based on a lack of understanding, the dance was banned until reinstated by King Kalakaua in the 1880s.

Within the last 25 years Hawai'i has experienced a renaissance of both *kahiko*, or ancient, and *'auana*, or modern, *hula*. People of all races now join Hawaiians in *hula* festivals throughout Hawai'i, including the Merry Monarch, King Kamehameha, and Keiki Hula. New festivals are emerging in Hawai'i, as well as on the mainland and even in countries as far away as Japan.

The *hula*'s alluring magic continues to endure. *A Pocket Guide to How to Hula* has been created to help people of all ages to learn to dance and enjoy the *hula*. The songs included are visitor's favorites comprised of *hapa haole* songs, written originally in English. Popular during the thirties, forties and fifties, they are still requested today.

So get ready to feel beautiful, and be a part of the rain, wind, and warm sun of Hawai'i as you learn to use your lovely *hula* hands with grace. Discover a new way to celebrate life—learn to dance the *hula!*

Patricia Lei Anderson Murray

How to use this book

This book uses step-by-step photographs and written instructions to teach the *hula*. The photographs show the main positions, while the captions provide the song lyrics, the footwork, and hand motions.

Dancers who use this book will find it very worthwhile to learn basic foot movements first, then fit the hand motions into the rhythm. In many cases, the dance is best learned by phrases.

For example, when doing "Lovely Hula Hands," review steps 1, 2, and 3 and see how they flow together from one motion to another. Learn the footwork first, without trying the hands. Then work through the hand movements. Finally, put both the hands and feet together. Learning by phrases will help you remember the story you are telling.

So, take your time with each dance. Feel the poetry of the movements and how they relate to the lyrics. And, above all, have fun.

*B*asic Footwork

To dance the *hula,* you must have some idea of the basic steps and hand motions. Grace and coordination come with practice and desire. Good dancers feel the rhythm of the music and move naturally with it. Shoulders should be relaxed, back straight, and knees slightly bent, arms and fingers moving gracefully.

Here is a footwork glossary of basic foot patterns generally used in *hula.* Note that not all of the movements will be used in each song. We have chosen to use the simplest patterns.

kaholo: The most important *hula* step is the *kaholo,* (once referred to as the "vamp"). *Kaholo* is the most often used step, whether it be side to side, front to back, or diagonally. A *kaholo* is more of a sliding step, rather than lifting the foot as you move.

kaholo right: Right foot takes a short step to the right. Bring left foot beside the right. Take another step to the right, then bring the left foot next to it and hold.
Right, left, right, hold. 4 counts.

Kaholo Right

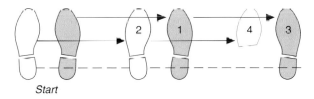

Start

kaholo left: Left foot takes a short step to the left. Right foot follows. The pattern is repeated on the left in the same manner as it was on the right.

Left, right, left, hold. 4 counts.

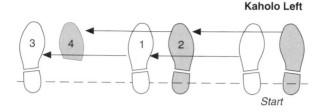

Kaholo Left

ka'o: Sway hips by shifting weight to the right side and lifting left heel. Then shift weight to the left side and lift right heel. Sways are usually done in 2 or 4 counts.

Ka'o

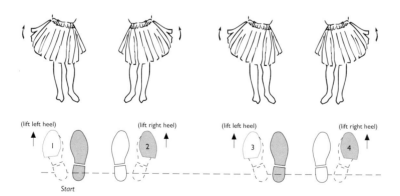

lele: Step right,
then left,
either forward
or back.
2 counts each side.

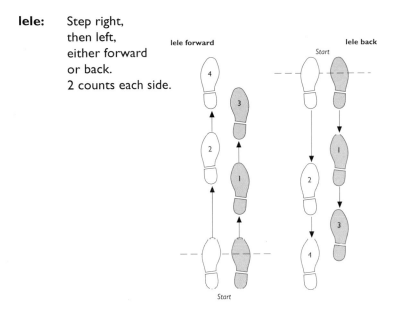

hela: Point right foot forward, bring back, then point left foot forward, then bring back. *Hela* can be done in 2 or 4 counts.

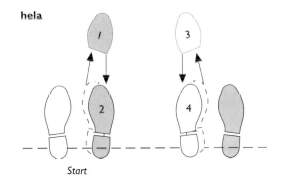

'ami: Right—rotate hips counterclockwise, one rotation for each count. Left—rotate hips clockwise. Bent knees make the 'ami easier.

'ami

Right   Left

around the island: Step on the right foot. Do one complete 'ami. Pivot on the left foot. Repeat three more 'ami while moving in a circle to face front again.

around the island

Start

holoholo: Slide **8** steps to the right (four counts), then **8** steps to the left.

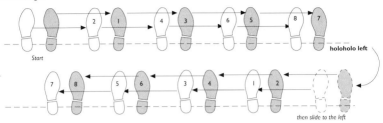

holoholo right

Start

holoholo left

then slide to the left

'uwehe: Step on right foot, then lift both heels and push knees slightly apart. Step left, repeat same movements on the left. Shoulders should not move when heels are lifted. 2 counts for each 'uwehe.

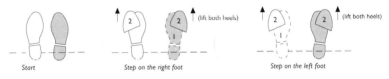

'uwehe

Start

Step on the right foot

(lift both heels)

Step on the left foot

(lift both heels)

lele 'uwehe: Step to right, brush foot forward, bring back and lift heels. Step left, repeat same steps, going left.

lele 'uwehe

Start

Step on right foot

(lift both heels)

Step on left foot

(lift both heels)

*B*asic Hand Motions

Graceful hands tell the story, but the dance is most beautiful when it is enjoyed by the dancer as well as the audience. A good dancer visualizes what she describes—the mountains are cool and high, the flowers fresh and fragrant—when she knows her story, her *hula* can be truly enjoyed by all.

Here are some basic *hula* hand motions that are used often.

Let's go to the ocean
hands gently beat up and down showing the rhythm of the waves

And watch the tide roll in
hands continually roll over each other to show the rolling sea

The swaying palms
left arm becomes the land, right arm and fingers sway showing a waving palm

And the swirling winds.
left hand forward while right hand circles twice over head

The rising sun
start at the knees, both hands part and rise above the head to shape the sun

The clouds rolling by
hands continue to roll over head moving from one side to the other

The colors of the rainbow
palms meet at the left...right hand lifts and shapes an arching rainbow

And the stars in the sky
both hands meet over head; two fingers of each hand cross to shape the stars

Let's go to the mountains
right hand higher than the left shaping mountain cliffs

The valleys low
right hand up and left hand gracefully moving down to feet, for valley

I'll sing you a song
hand gracefully gesturing at mouth for song

Of long ago
hands cross at chest, then open to extend out

I'll weave you a lei
left hand up holding a flower, right hand using a needle to string a lei

For you to wear
both hands above head, coming down at neck to show the wearing of a lei

And gather flowers
finger tips closed and pointing downward; wrists turn upward as flower blooms

For your hair.
hands gesturing to the left to show flowers in the hair

This is our story
hands at mouth to tell story or to sing a song

Our hands can tell
hands at chest level and gracefully alternating, one on top the other

Of our island home
palms inward at waist, extend side ways, wrists turn, palms face outward, fingers come together to shape an island

That we love so well.
hands cross at chest to show embracing love

The Songs

The Hukilau Song
by Jack Owens, Copyright renewed 1976 and
assigned to Owens-Kemp Music Co. (ASCAP)

Oh, we're going to a hukilau,
A huki, huki, huki, huki, hukilau.
Everybody loves a hukilau,
Where the laulau is the kaukau at the
    hukilau.
We throw our nets out into the sea,
And all the 'ama'ama come swimming to
    me.
Oh, we're going to a hukilau,
Huki, huki, huki, huki, hukilau.
What a beautiful day for fishing,
The old Hawaiian way,
And the hukilau nets are swishing,
Down in old La'ie Bay.
Oh, we're going to a hukilau,
Huki, huki, huki, huki, hukilau.

Lovely Hula Hands
Written by Alex Anderson, Copyright ©1940
PolyGram International Publishing, Inc.

Lovely hula hands,
Graceful as the birds in motion,
Gliding like the gulls over the ocean,
Lovely hula hands,
Kou lima nani e.
Lovely hula hands,
Telling of the rain in the valley,
And the swirling winds over the pali,
Lovely hula hands,
Kou lima nani e.
I can feel the soft caresses of your hula
    hands,
Your lovely hula hands.
Every little move expresses so I'll under-
    stand,
All the tender meaning of your hula
    hands,

Fingertips that say, "Aloha,"
Say to me again, "I love you,"
Lovely hula hands,
Kou lima nani e.

Little Brown Gal
by Johnny Noble, Lee Wood and Don
McDiarmid
©Copyright 1935 by Bourne Co.

It's not the islands fair that are calling to
    me,
Not the balmy air not the tropical sea,
But it's a little brown gal, in a little grass
    skirt,
In a little grass shack, in Hawaii.
It isn't Waikiki nor Kamehameha's pali,
Not the beach boys free, with their
    ho'omalimali,
It's a little brown gal, in a little grass skirt,
In a little grass shack in Hawaii.
Through that island wonderland,
She's broken all the kane's hearts.
It's not hard to understand,
For that wahine is a gal of parts.
I'll be leaving soon, but the thrill I'll en-
    joy,
Is not the island moon, or the fish and
    the poi,
It's just a little brown gal, in a little grass
    skirt,
In a little grass shack in Hawaii.

Sweet Leilani
by Harry Owens, Copyright 1935 Royal Music
Publisher

Sweet Leilani, heavenly flower,
Nature fashioned roses kissed with dew,
And then she placed them in a bower,
It was the start of you.
Sweet Leilani, heavenly flower,
I dreamed of paradise for two,
You are my paradise completed,
You are my dreams come true.

Sweet Leilani, heavenly flower,
Tropic skies are jealous as they shine,
I think they're jealous of your blue eyes,
Jealous because you're mine.
Sweet Leilani, heavenly flower,
I dreamed of paradise for two,
You are my paradise completed,
You are my dreams come true.

Hawaiian Hospitality

by Harry Owens and Ray Kinney. Copyright 1938 Royal Music Publisher

Along the beach at Waikiki,
A fair wahine is waiting for me,
With her dark eyes and lovable charms,
And very sweet Hawaiian hospitality.
Beneath the moon we stroll along,
And life is just like a beautiful song,
When she whispers, "Come into my arms,"
It's just the old Hawaiian hospitality.
And though my heart may sob to "Aloha" when I sail away,
How my heart will throb to the thought of coming back some day.
And when my dreams of love come true,
There will be 'okolehao for two,
A little wela ka hao might do.
It's just the old Hawaiian hospitality.

To You, Sweetheart, Aloha

by Harry Owens. Copyright 1937 Royal Music Publisher

To you, sweetheart, aloha,
Aloha from the bottom of my heart.
Keep the smile on your lips,
Brush the tears from your eye.
One more aloha,
Then it's time for good bye.

To you, sweetheart, aloha,
In dreams I'll be with you, dear, tonight,
And I'll pray for that day when
We two will meet again.
Until then, sweetheart, aloha.

Hawaiian Wedding Song

by Al Hoffman, Dick Manning and Charles E. King. Copyright © 1926, 1958 (Renewed) by Charles E. King Music Co., MCA Music Publishing, a div. of MCA Inc. & Al Hoffman Songs, Inc., c/o Music Sales Corporation

This is the moment I've waited for,
I can hear my heart singing,
Soon bells will be ringing.

This is the moment of sweet aloha,
I will love you longer than forever,
Promise me that you will leave me never.

Here and now, dear,
All my love I vow, dear,
I will love you longer than forever,
Promise me that you will leave me never

Now that we are one,
Clouds won't hide the sun,
Blue skies of Hawaii smile on this our wedding day!

I do love you,
With all my heart.

Here and now, dear,
All my love I vow, dear.
I will love you longer than forever,
Promise me that you will leave me never.

Now that we are one
Clouds won't hide the sun
Blue skies of Hawaii smile on this our wedding day!
I do love you,
With all my heart.
With all my heart.

The Hukilau Song

by Jack Owens

The old Hawaiian way of fishing is to lay out the long nets in the ocean in the evening, and in the morning the whole community would come and help pull the nets in. This fun song tells of this favorite way of fishing—the *hukilau*.

1 **Oh, we're going**
Kaholo right. Right thumb
hitching, left hand on hip.

2 **to a hukilau**
Kaholo left. Pull nets two times
from the right to the left.

3 **a huki, huki, huki, huki,**
Kaholo right.
Pull two times left to the right.
hukilau
Kaholo left. Pulling nets two times
from right to left.

4 **Everybody**
Kaholo right. Palms up and out.

5 **loves a hukilau**
Kaholo left. Pull nets two times
from the right to left.

6 **Where the laulau**
Ka'o right. Left palm up, dip right
two fingers into the palm.

9 **We throw our nets**
Kaholo left. Throw from right
shoulder over to ocean on left.

10 **out into the sea**
Kaholo right.
Ocean motion.

7 **is the kaukau**
Ka'o left. Bring same fingers to mouth to taste the food.

8 **at the hukilau**
Kaholo right. Pull nets two times left to two times right.

11 **And all the 'ama 'ama**
Ka'o right, left. Right hand over left with thumbs moving as fins.

12 **come swimming to me**
Four small ka'o, dipping. Hands the same.

13 **Oh, we're going**
Kaholo right. Right thumb
hitching, left hand on hip.
(step 1)

14 **to a hukilau**
Kaholo left. Pull nets two times
from the right to the left.
(step 2)

17 **for fishing**
Kaholo left. Throw nets from
right shoulder to ocean on left.

18 **the old Hawaiian way**
Ka'o four times.
Hands from self out.

15 **a huki, huki, huki, huki,**
Kaholo right. Pull two times left to the right.
hukilau
Kaholo left. Pulling nets two times from right to left. (step 3)

16 **What a beautiful day**
Kaholo right. Hands open above head.

19 **And the hukilau nets are swishing**
Kaholo right, left. Swish hands twice on the left, then on right.

20 **down in old La'ie Bay**
Side kaholo stepping on the right. Left hand up, right palm up, at waist, turn then reverse motion, and repeat.

21 **Oh, we're going**
Kaholo right. Right thumb
hitching, left hand on hip.
(same as step 1)

22 **to a hukilau**
Kaholo left. Pull nets two times
from the right to the left.
(same as step 2)

25 **loves a hukilau**
Kaholo left. Pull nets two times
from the right to the left.
(same as step 5)

26 **Where the laulau**
Ka'o right. Left palm up, dip
right two fingers into the palm.
(same as step 6)

23 **a huki, huki, huki, huki,**
Kaholo right. Pull two times left to the right.
hukilau
Kaholo left. Pulling nets two times from right to left.
(same as step 3)

24 **Everybody**
Kaholo right. Palms up and out.
(same as step 4)

27 **is the kaukau**
Ka'o left. Bring same fingers to mouth to taste the food.
(same as step 7)

28 **at the hukilau**
Kaholo right. Pull left to right.
(same as step 8)

 29 **We throw our nets**
Kaholo left. Throw from right shoulder over to ocean on left. (same as step 9)

 30 **out into the sea**
Kaholo right. Ocean motion. (same as step 10)

33 **Oh, we're going**
Kaholo right. Right thumb hitching, left on hip. (same as step 1)

 34 **to a hukilau**
Kaholo left. Pull nets two times from the right to the left (same as step 2)

31 **And all the 'ama 'ama**
Ka'o right, left. Right hand over left with thumbs moving as fins. (same as step 11)

32 **come swimming to me**
Four small ka'o, dipping. Hands the same. (same as step 12)

35 **a huki, huki, huki,**
Kaholo right.
huki, huki, huki,
Kaholo left.
huki, huki, huki...
Kaholo right. (same as step 3)

36 **hukilau**
On final hukilau—step back with left foot, point right foot. Hands come together and extend over pointed foot. Bow from waist.

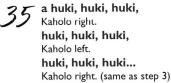

Lovely Hula Hands

by R. Alex Anderson

"Lovely Hula Hands" is one of the most romantic hulas and quite easy to learn. The motions let you glide as a seagull, tell of rain and swirling winds and feel the caress of love all in one dance.

1 **Lovely hula hands**
Kaholo right. Gracefully extend hands upward right, palms out. (hula hands position)

2 **Graceful as the birds in**
Kaholo left. Repeat motions on the left.

3 **motion**
Kaholo right. Finger tips on shoulders, then extended in a wing motion. Kaholo left. Repeat motions on the left.

4 **Gliding like the gulls**
Ka'o right to left. Stay in winged position, dipping in sway.

5 **over the ocean**
Kaholo right. Hands rolling one
over the other as the waves do.

6 **Lovely Hula Hands**
Kaholo left. Gracefully extend
hands upward right, palms out.
(hula hands position)

9 **Telling of the rain**
Kaholo left. Both hands swooping
upward from the right to the left.

10 **in the valley**
Kaholo right. Sprinkling raindrops
down from the left to the right.
Kaholo left. Repeat motions from
right to left.

7 **Kou lima nani e**
Ka'o right, then left.
Repeat same hands on the left.

8 **Lovely hula hands**
Kaholo right. Hands at hula
position to the right.

11 **And the swirling winds**
Kaholo right. Left hand out,
right hand circling head 2 times

12 **over the pali**
Kaholo left. Left hand up,
right fingers touching left palm.

13 **Lovely hula hands**
Kaholo right, hula hands position.

14 **Kou lima nani e**
Kaholo left. Hands upward on
the left, palms facing you.

17 **Your lovely hula hands**
Kaholo Left. Hula hands
position.

18 **Every little move**
'Ami right two counts.
Left hand on hip, right hand at
chest looking over right
shoulder.

15 **I can feel the soft caresses**
Kaʻo four counts from right to left.
Hands crossed at chest, fingers
moving up and down gently along
arms.

16 **of your hula hands**
Kaholo right.
Hula hands position.

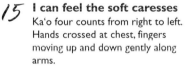

19 **expresses**
ʻAmi left two counts.
Switch hands and repeat
motion. Looking over left
shoulder.

20 **So I'll understand**
Kaholo right. Right index finger
at temple, left index finger at
right elbow.

21 **All the tender meaning**
Kaholo left. Fold palms up then open up front.

22 **of your hula hands**
Kaholo right. Hula hands position.

25 **Say to me again**
Ka'o left, right. Hands from mouth to self.

26 **I love you**
Kaholo left. Hands come from sides to cross and embrace.

23 **Fingertips that say**
Ka'o left, right. Hands
gracefully moving left over
right, right over left.

24 **Aloha**
Kaholo left. Hands from mouth
out. Kaholo right. Hands open.

27 **Lovely hula hands**
Kaholo right. Hula hands
position.

28 **Kou lima nani e**
Step back on left foot, point
right foot. Hands upward on
left, palms up facing outward.
Bow—open hands to shoulder
level, palms down, keep foot in
same position —bow.

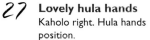

Little brown Gal

Words and music by Lee Wood, Don McDiarmid and Johnny Noble

A great favorite, this simple *hula* about a Hawaiian sweetheart is among the first requested at any gathering. The motions tell the story well, and *kama'aina* find this a great one to teach to *malihini* friends.

1 **It's not the islands fair**
Kaholo right. Left hand up,
right hand, palm down moving
across the body from left to right.

2 **that are calling to me**
Kaholo left. Left hand to mouth,
right hand extended forward,
then both hands to me.

3 **Not the balmy air**
Kaholo right. Left hand out, right
hand circling two times over
head.

4 **not the tropical sea**
Kaholo left. Ocean motion.

5 **It's a little brown gal**
Kaholo right. From overhead,
outline self.

6 **in a little grass skirt**
Kaholo left. Swish skirt with both
hands.

9 **It isn't Waikiki**
Kaholo right. Ocean motion.

10 **nor Kamehameha's pali**
Kaholo left. Hands form cliffs.

7 **in a little grass shack**
Kaholo right.
Form a roof with hands.

8 **in Hawaii**
Kaholo left. Right hand up. Left
hand palm down moving across
the body from right to left.

11 **Not the beach boys free**
Step forward right once,
left once. Point right hand first
then left

12 **with their hoʻomalimali**
ʻAmi 2 times. Cross arms and
stroke upper arms with fingers.

13 **It's a little brown gal**
Kaholo right. From overhead,
outline self. (same as step 5)

14 **in a little grass skirt**
Kaholo left. Swish skirt with both
hands. (same as step 6)

17 **Through that**
Steps 17 through 19 form one
motion. Take four steps in
"Around the Island" motion,
starting with right foot. Point
left hand up.

18 **island**
Second of four steps.
Alternate hand positions.

15 **in a little grass shack**
Kaholo right. Form a roof with hands (same as step 7)

16 **in Hawaii**
Kaholo left. Right hand up. Left hand palm down moving across the body from right to left. (same as step 8)

19 **wonderland**
Last of four steps.
Continue alternate positions.

20 **She's broken all the kane's**
Kaholo right. Clench fists by heart to show something being broken two times.

21 **hearts**
Kaholo left. Turn palms to face each other.

22 **It's not hard**
Kaholo right. Left hand on hip, right hand forward shaking finger two times.

25 **wahine is a**
Step forward left foot. Point with left hand, then clap.

26 **gal of parts**
Ka'o two times. From over head, outline self.

23 **to understand**
Kaholo Left. Right index finger at temple, left index at right elbow.

24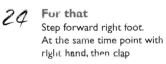
For that
Step forward right foot. At the same time point with right hand, then clap

27 **I'll be leaving soon**
Kaholo right. Right hand up, left hand extended to left.

28 **but the thrill I'll enjoy**
Kaholo left. Embrace motion.

29 **is not the island moon**
Kaholo right. Hands start to shape the moon from knees and rise.

30 **or the fish and the poi**
Kaholo left. Left hand palm up, right hand two fingers dip into left palm, then to mouth.

33 **in a little grass shack**
Kaholo right. Form a roof with hands. (same as step 7)

34 **in Hawaii**
Kaholo left. Right hand up. Left hand palm down moving across the body from right to left. (same as step 8)

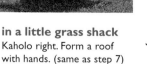

31 **It's a little brown gal**
Kaholo right. From overhead, outline self. (same as step 5)

32 **in a little grass skirt**
Kaholo left. Swish skirt with both hands. (same as step 6)

35 **Pau.**
Point right foot forward, hands meet, head slightly bowed.

Sweet Leilani

by Harry Owens

*S*weet Leilani was symbolic of beauty, grace and paradise come true. She caused a stir, however, because of her blue eyes and therein lies the intrigue of this favorite song.

1 **Sweet Leilani**
Ka'o right, left. Hands at head then gracefully move down to hips.

2 **heavenly flower**
Point right foot. Hands pick flower, and hold up on right side.

3 **Nature fashioned roses kissed with dew**
Kaholo right. Hands sprinkling rain from right down to left. Kaholo left. Repeat rain from left to right.

4 **and then she placed them in a bower**
Kaholo right. Left hand up, right hand palm down moving from left to right. Kaholo left. Repeat motion on opposite side.

5
It was the start of you
Kaholo right. Hands from self, forward, palms up. Kaholo left. Pointing to left, palms down, motioning "you".

6
Sweet Leilani
Ka'o right, left.
Hands at head then gracefully move down to hips

9
for two
Kaholo right. Two fingers showing with right hand, left hand on hip.

10
You are my paradise
Ka'o left, right. Hands pointing to right.

7 **heavenly flower**
Kaholo right. Hands pick flower
and shape bud.

8 **I dreamed of paradise**
Kaholo left. Palms together at
right temple for "dreamed."

11 **completed**
Kaholo left. Open hands cross
over chest in embrace.

12 **You are my dreams
come true**
Kaholo right. Hands in dream
position. Kaholo left. Hands
open from self and out.

13 Sweet Leilani
Ka'o right, left. Hands at head then gracefully move to hips.

14 heavenly flower
Kaholo right. Hands pick flower and shape bud

17 blue eyes
Hela left, right. Motion to eyes.

18 jealous because you're mine
Kaholo left. Right hand on hip, left arm over chest, looking over left shoulder. Ka'o right, left. Repeat motion on opposite side.

15 Tropic skies are jealous as they shine
Kaholo left. Hands move above head from right to left for rolling clouds. Kaholo right. Continue motion.

16 I think they're jealous of your
Hela left, right. Think motion.

19 Sweet Leilani
Ka'o right, left. Hands at head then gracefully move to hips.

20 heavenly flower
Kaholo right. Hands pick flower and shape bud.

21 **I dreamed of paradise**
Kaholo left. Hands in dream position.

22 **for two**
Ka'o right, left. Two fingers, right hand, left hand on hip.

25 **you are my dreams**
Kaholo right. Hands at dream position.

26 **come true**
Step back on left foot, point right foot... Hands come from self forward and open, palms up, palms down...

23 You are my paradise
Kaholo right. Hands pointing to right.

24 completed
Kaholo left. Hands open and cross over chest in embrace.

27 …and bow.

Hawaiian Hospitality

Words and music by Harry Owens and Ray Kinney

The charms of a beautiful Hawaiian woman are described in this happy *hula*. Moments spent together were precious memories and he longed for the thought of coming back some day.

1 **Along the Beach**
Step forward right foot.
Hands to left, palms down.

2 **At Wai...**
Step left. Repeat hands to the right.

3 **...kiki**
Kaholo right. Ocean motion.

4 **A fair wahine is waiting**
Kaholo left. From overhead, outline self.

5 **for me**
Ka'o two times. Right index finger at temple, left index at right elbow.

6 **With her dark eyes**
Kaholo right. Hands at eyes. Palms in, then out.

9 **Hawaiian Hospitality**
'Ami, left two times. Alternate arms of last motion.

10 **Beneath the moon we stroll along**
Kaholo right, then left. Shape moon starting at knees and rise.

7 **and lovable charms**
Kaholo left. Embrace motion.

8 **and very sweet**
'Ami, right two times. Right arm
at chest, left hand at hip.

11 **And life is just like a**
beautiful
Kaholo right. Arms reach out in
front.

12 **song**
Kaholo left. Hands mouth out.

13 **When she whispers**
Ka'o two times. Right hand up, left index finger at lips, then out.

14 **Come into my arms**
Ka'o two times. Embrace motion.

16 **And though my heart**
Kaholo right. Turn palms to face each other.

17 **may sob to**
Kaholo left. Reverse palms gracefully.

15 **It's just the old Hawaiian Hospitality**
'Ami right twice, then left twice. Right arm at chest, left arm on hip…

…left arm at chest, right on hip.

18 **Aloha**
Kaholo forward right. Mouth out.

19 **When I sail away**
Kaholo forward left. Fingertips shape a boat and dip in water two times.

 20 **How my heart**
Ka'o two times. Turn palms to
face each other.

21 **will throb to the thought**
Ka'o two times. Reverse palms
gracefully.

23 **some day**
Kaholo right forward.
Hands out.

24 **And when my dreams**
Ka'o once. Dream motion.

22 **of coming back**
Step back with right foot.
Beckon on left. Step back with
right foot. Beckon on left.

Step back with left foot. Beckon on
right.

25 **of love**
Ka'o once. Embrace motion.

26 **come true**
Kaholo left. Extend hands
forward and open.

27 **There will be okolehao**
Ka'o two times. Dip and arms sweep up to hold drink to lips.

28 **for two**
Kaholo right. Right hands holds up two fingers, left on hip.

31 **hao**
On third step which is left foot, click fingers.

32 **might do**
Kaholo right. Hands open out front.

29 **A little wela...**
Kaholo left. On first step to the left, slap skirt.

30 **ika...**
On second step which is right foot, clap hands.

33 **It's just the old Hawaiian Hospitality**
Ami two times to the right, then 'ami two times to the left.

34 Step back on the left foot. Right foot pointed and bow.

5 **from the bottom of my**
Kaholo left. Continue motion
until hands are outstretched.

6 **heart**
Ka'o for 4 counts. Right, left,
right, left. Hands roll at heart.

9 **Brush the tears from your**
Kaholo right. Gently brush tears.

10 **eye**
Kaholo left. Palms out at eyes.

7 **Keep the smile on your**
Kaholo right. Hands to smile, palms in.

8 **lips**
Kaholo left. Turn hands outward at face.

11 **One more**
Kaholo right. Left hand on hip, right hand pointing.

12 **aloha**
Kaholo left. Arms cross for embrace.

13 **Then it's time for good bye**
Kaholo right. Right arm over
chest, left on hip. Kaholo left.
Repeat motion on opposite side.

14 **To you,**
Kaholo right. Hands pointing to
right (same as step 1)

17 **In dreams I'll be with you
dear**
Ka'o four counts. Right, left,
right, left. Slowly come to dream
position at right temple.

18 **tonight**
Kaholo right, left. Hands over
head, gently cross, then open.

15 **sweetheart,**
Kaholo left. Cross arms at chest, looking over left shoulder. (same as step 2)

16 **aloha**
Kaholo right. Left hand up, right hand from mouth out to right. Kaholo left. Repeat opposite motion on left.
(same as step 3)

19 **And I'll pray for that day**
Kaholo right. Prayer position.

20 **when**
Kaholo left. Hands open from self forward.

21 **We two will meet**
Ka'o right, left. Two fingers on right hand, left hand on hip.

22 **again**
Kaholo right. Hands clasp up front.

25 **aloha**
Kaholo right. Left hand up, right hand from mouth out to right

26 Step back on left foot, hands open, palms down, and bow.

 Until then
Kaholo left. Hands from self
forward and open.

 **sweetheart**
Kaholo right. Hands open and
crossing to embrace.

The Hawaiian Wedding Song

by Al Hoffman, Dick Manning and Charles E. King

The "Hawaiian Wedding Song" is such a special part of an island wedding. You can make your wedding day special by learning this *hula* and dancing it for your sweetheart. Make a dream come true with the "Hawaiian Wedding Song."

1 **This is**
Kaholo right. Palms up from self forward.

2 **the moment**
Ka'o left, right Palms down, together then out.

3 **I've waited for**
Kaholo left. Left hand at chest, right hand down to side, looking over right shoulder. Kaholo right. Reverse hands, looking over the left shoulder.

4 **I can hear**
Kaholo left. Left hand opened at ear, right hand moving from ear out.

5   **my heart singing**
Ka'o right, left. Hands roll twice
at the heart.

6   **Soon bells**
Step right, then left in a circle.
Left hand up, right hand at chest, then
alternate hands in bell ringing motion.

9   **the moment**
Kaholo left. Palms down, together
then out.

10   **of sweet aloha**
Ka'o four counts, right to left.
Arms out, cross to embrace.

7 **will be ringing**
...ringing bells for four counts.

8 **This is**
Kaholo right. Palms up from self forward.

11 **I will love you longer**
Kaholo right. Hands to self, then cross to embrace.

12 **than forever**
Kaholo left. I lands scoop down, cross, and open above head.

13 **Promise me that you will leave me**
Ka'o right, left. Hands from self, then out to right side.

14 **never**
Kaholo right. Left hand on hip, right finger gesturing "never."

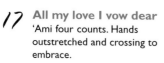

17 **All my love I vow dear**
'Ami four counts. Hands outstretched and crossing to embrace.

18 **I will love you longer**
Kaholo right. Hands to self, then cross to embrace.

15 **Here and**
Lele left, then lele right.
Right hand to chest, left hand
forward, alternate hands on lele.

16 **now dear**
Kaholo left. Open hands, palms
up.

19 **than forever.**
Kaholo left. Hands scoop
down, cross, and open above
head.

20 **Promise me that you will
leave me**
Ka'o right, left. Hands from self,
then out to right side.

21 **never**
Kaholo right. Left hand on hip, right finger gesturing "never."

22 **Now that we are**
Kaholo left. Arms outstretched and coming together, palms up.

25 **the sun**
Dip as you kaholo left Shape the sun starting at the knees and rise overhead.

26 **Blue skies of**
Kaholo right. Hands cross above head and open for the skies.

23 one
Ka'o right, left. Clasp hands
forward on right ka'o, then at
heart on left ka'o.

24 Clouds won't hide
Kaholo right. Roll hands
above head from left to right.

27 Hawaii smile on
Kaholo left. Right hand up.
Left hand, palm up, show land
from right to left.

28 this our
Step right, then left beginning to
move in a circle. Right hand at
chest, left hand up, alternating for
four counts.

29 **wedding day!**
Continue motions
to complete the circle.

30 **I do**
Kaholo right. Hands at mouth
and out.

33 **heart**
Dipped ka'o, left, right two
counts. Roll hands at heart for
two counts.

34 **Here and**
Lele left, then lele right. Right
hand to chest, left hand
forward, alternate hands on
lele. (same as step 15)

31 **love you**
Kaholo left. Love motion then point to the left.

32 **With all my**
Kaholo right. Left hand at heart, right hand sweeps from side to bosom.

35 **now dear**
Kaholo left. Open hands, palms up. (same as step 16)

36 **All my love I vow dear**
'Ami four counts. Hands outstretched and crossing to embrace. (same as step 17)

37 **I will love you longer**
Kaholo right. Hands to self,
then cross to embrace.
(same as step 18)

38 **than forever.**
Kaholo left. Hands scoop down,
cross, and open above head.
(same as step 19)

41 **Now that we are**
Kaholo left. Arms outstretched
and coming together, palms up.
(same as step 22)

42 **one**
Ka'o right, left. Clasp hands
forward on right ka'o, then at
heart on left ka'o.
(same as step 23)

39 **Promise me that you will leave me**
Ka'o right, left. Hands from self, then out to right side. (same as step 20)

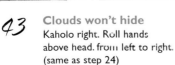

40 **never**
Kaholo right. Left hand on hip, right finger gesturing "never." (same as step 21)

43 **Clouds won't hide**
Kaholo right. Roll hands above head. from left to right. (same as step 24)

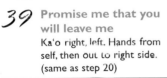

44 **the sun**
Dip as you kaholo left. Shape the sun starting at the knees and rise overhead. (same as step 25)

 Blue skies of
Kaholo right.
Hands cross above head and
open for the skies.
(same as step 26)

46 **Hawaii smile on**
Kaholo left.
Right hand up.
Left hand, palm up, show land
from right to left.
(same as step 27)

49 **I do**
Kaholo right. Hands at mouth
and out. (same as step 30)

50 **love you**
Kaholo left. Love motion then
point to the left.
(same as step 31)

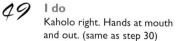

47 **this our**
Step right, then left beginning to move in a circle. Right hand at chest, left hand up, alternating for four counts.
(same as step 28)

48 **wedding day!**
Continue motions to complete the circle. (same as step 29)

51 **With all my**
Kaholo right. Left hand at heart, right hand sweeps from side to bosom.
(same as step 32)

52 **heart**
Dipped ka'o, left, right two counts. Roll hands at heart for two counts.
(same step as 33)

53

With all my
Kaholo left. Left hand at
heart, right hand sweeps from
side to bosom.
(same as step 32)

54

heart
Dipped ka'o, right, left two counts.
Roll hands at heart for two counts.
(same step as 33)
To complete song, step back on left
foot. Point right foot and bow.

lossary

aloha — love, hello, goodbye
'ama 'ama — mullet
'auana — to dance freely
'awapuhi — ginger blossom
'okolehao — delicious drink
'opu — belly
ha'ina 'ia mai ana ka puana — "this is the story I tell"
halau — school
ho'omalimali — to flatter
huki — to pull
hukilau — pull fish nets in
hula — Hawaiian dance
kahiko — ancient
kama'aina — native-born
Kamehameha—referring to the king
kane — man, boy

kau kau — slang word for food
kou lima nani e — your lovely hands
kumu hula — hula teacher
La'ie Bay — North Shore on O'ahu
lau lau — food wrapped in taro leaves and tied in ti leaves
lei — garland of flowers
malihini — newcomer
pali — cliff
pau — finished
poi — pounded cooked taro
Waikiki — famous beach on O'ahu
wahine — woman, girl
wela ka hau — "have a good time"

iographies

Briana Kaluhinano Smits began performing at the early age of seven, and loves all performing arts. She has participated in many hula competitions placing first or second in solo categories. She is a proud member of the award winning *halau*, Na 'Opio o Ko'olau— *kumu hula:* Michael and James Dela Cruz.

Briana has also performed in musical presentations at The Ronald E. Bright Performing Arts Center. She is an honor student at her school, and active in student government.

Amber Kamailelauli'i Murray is a graduate of Kamehameha School and presently a student in Education and Hawaiian Studies at the Kap'iolani Community College.

Her love of *hula* began at a young age under *kumu hula,* Olana Ai, and continues to grow through her Hawaiian Studies Program. Amber and her *halau* "Na Wa'a Eo 'O Kahiki" have just returned from a cultural exchange to New Zealand, where they shared traditions, language, and dance. Presently, she dances at the Hilton Hawaiian Village Hotel in Waikiki.

Joe Perrone has been a photographer for 25 years, photographing freelance and under contract which involves shooting on location and in the studio. He has photographed many Hawaiian style shows as part of a review for local publications and has captured the graceful movements of hundreds of dancers during special events such as weddings, parties and conventions.

Patricia Lei Anderson Murray has been a lifelong ambassador of Hawai'i and the tradition of *aloha.* For years she was well known in our island community as a former Miss Hawaii and a talented finalist in the Miss America pageant, but her influence did not stop there. She has traveled throughout the world as a singer, and dancer; performing in London, New York, Australia, and the Orient. Hula has always been a happy part of her life. Her *kumu hula* were Alicia Smith, and Maiki Aiu Lake. She shares this love of *hula* in her recently produced "Hula for Health" and "How to Hula" videos.

Presently she is a Corporate Training Consultant in Time Management for the Franklin Quest Co., and a partner along with select artists and crafters at "Native Books and Beautiful Things," a Hawaiian store that specializes in culture, art and *aloha.* She is an author, songwriter and motivational speaker who has graced many stages in government as well as professional and private arenas.

Patricia is also active in her community, serving as president of the Board of Directors of the Domestic Violence Clearing House and Legal Hotline, and Vice President of the Kalihi-Palama Culture and Arts Society, which sponsors the Keiki Hula Festival. She is married to Harry Murray Jr. and together they have five children and four grandchildren. Amber Kamailelauli'i is the youngest of the five Murrays. Each of the Murrays specializes in some area of performing arts.